WEST GLAMORGAN
COUNTY LIBRARY
SCHOOL LIBRARY &
RESOURCES SERVICE

WITHDRAWN

KT-425-433

2100151631

E.L.R.S.

WITHDRAWN

HOW THEY LIVED

AN EDWARDIAN HOUSEHOLD

STEWART ROSS

Illustrated by
John James

Wayland

(5)

S222143   942·082

How They Lived

First published in 1986 by
Wayland (Publishers) Limited
61 Western Road, Hove
East Sussex BN3 1JD, England

© Copyright 1986 Wayland (Publishers) Limited

British Library Cataloguing in Publication Data
Ross, Stewart
An Edwardian household. — (How They Lived)
1. England — Social life and customs — 20th century
I. Title   II. James, John, *1959-*   III. Series
942.0823   DA566.4

ISBN 0 85078 621 5

Typeset by Planagraphic Typesetters Limited
Printed in Italy by G. Canale & C.S.p.A., Turin
Bound in Great Britain by The Bath Press, Avon

CONTENTS

A DIFFICULT DAY

Things had not gone right all day. The master of the house, who had gone to bed late the night before, was woken at the crack of dawn by the milkman's singing. That put him in a bad mood. Nanny was grumpy because the baby had kept her awake most of the night.

At lunch the cook had burned the meat, and the soup was cold. Finally, at six o'clock, the kitchen maid dropped a tray full of the best china: the crash could be heard all over the house. The unfortunate girl was given a week's wages, told to pack her bags and leave the next morning. A large Edwardian household was a busy place in which there was little time for those who caused trouble.

King Edward VII (1901-10) came to the throne of Great Britain on the death of his mother, Queen Victoria. However, the phrase 'Edwardian Britain' usually refers to the period up to

Right *Inside a London slum house. The whole family lived and slept in this room.*

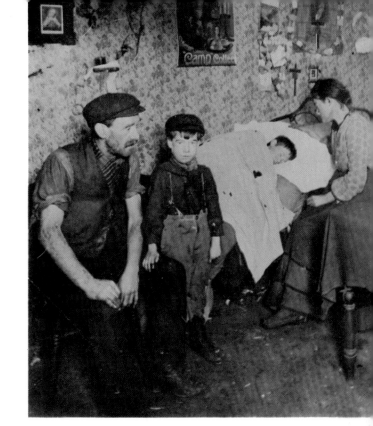

1914, when the First World War broke out and society changed almost beyond recognition.

The country was at peace for most of the Edwardian era, and it was richer than it had ever been before. Millions still lived in poverty, but for the well-off, life was very comfortable indeed. They built large houses, which were run by many servants: these households were more like little villages than homes.

THE CLASSES

The Edwardians were very aware of social class. The great majority belonged to the working class. The population of Britain in 1900 was about 35 million, of whom some 27 million were members of the working class. They earned wages of between 10 and 50 shillings a week (the equivalent today of between 50p and £2.50), and were employed to do manual labour. They spoke in the dialect of their region.

The middle classes liked to consider themselves 'respectable'. Women of the middle class rarely worked. The men were paid monthly, or ran their own businesses, and they never did manual work. The middle class was broad: a shopkeeper of the lower-middle class might earn £100 a year, while a London lawyer of the upper-middle class could earn over £2,000.

The tiniest social group was the upper class. This included the royal family, and the aristocratic and gentry families with inherited wealth. These titled people had no need to work. They spent lives of leisure, moving between their several houses, and spending almost what they wished from their considerable fortunes.

This book is not about the richest part of society, but about the middle and lower classes. These groups rarely mixed with each other, but a wealthy family might have employed as many as ten servants whom they could not ignore because they ran the house for them. So in a single house we can find a fair cross-section of Edwardian people all living under one roof.

These houses show how cramped living conditions were for the working class.

Right *Some working-class children resorted to theft when hungry.*

HOUSING

Between the palaces and stately homes of the very rich and the ghastly slums of the poor, there was a wide range of housing for the Edwardian middle classes. Many of them lived in rapidly-growing suburbs, where they moved to get away from the squalor of the inner cities. Men travelled to work each day by train or in an omnibus.

The less well-off lived in smaller terraced houses, two storeys high with small gardens at the front and rear.

Such families might be able to afford one servant, a maid, who would not live in the house but come in daily.

The wealthy built large detached houses of red brick, with stone lintels over the doors and windows. They were three storeys high, often with a basement too. The front door, sometimes enclosed by a porch decorated with tiles and stained glass, was used by the family and their guests. Servants and tradesmen used a back door.

For the family there were drawing rooms, a dining room, bedrooms and a bathroom, along with smaller sitting rooms and a study. Children had their separate nursery. The whole family used the wide front stairs.

The servants used the back stairs. Those who lived on the premises had their own small bedrooms at the top of the house or in the basement. The gardener might have his own cottage, while the butler, being the most important servant, had a little parlour of his own.

Grand old houses such as these, made comfortable homes for the Edwardian upper-middle class.

LIFE UPSTAIRS

A well-to-do lawyer and his wife were woken at about eight o'clock in the morning. It was not unusual for husbands and wives to have separate bedrooms and dressing rooms. They had no need of alarm clocks, for a maid, who had herself been awake since six, woke them with a tap on the bedroom door. Later she brought a pot of tea and biscuits.

The maid helped the lady of the house to dress, then the family met together for breakfast. The children had been dressed and brought down by nanny. Some families held morning prayers, led by the master of the house, which all the servants were supposed to attend.

Below *The mistress of the house expected her breakfast to be brought to her room every morning, so the maid had to be up early to prepare it.*

After breakfast the husband went off to work, the nanny took the children to their lessons, or back to the nursery, while the mistress of the house planned the day's meals with the cook. She then might pass the morning shopping with her maid, reading a book or playing games with her children.

The husband returned for lunch in the early afternoon, after which he went for a drive in his new car, while his wife rested. Visitors came to tea.

Motor cars gradually took the place of horse-drawn vehicles in the Edwardian period.

When they had gone, the parents said goodnight to their children, and talked with nanny about their behaviour during the day. After taking at least an hour over bathing and dressing, the lawyer and his wife took a cab to friends for dinner and bridge, leaving the servants to get the house ready for the morning.

11

A Servant's Lot

The life of a servant in an Edwardian household was tough. The worst paid was a maid, who was given food, lodging, a uniform and perhaps as little as £16 a year. Winter and summer she had to be up early to sweep the grates and light the fires. The rest of the day, which might last until eleven at night, was spent sweeping, scrubbing, fetching and carrying.

Servants usually had one half day off each week, when they could go out with friends. The lower servants, maids or men employed to do heavy jobs, were often badly treated. Not only were they ordered about by the family of the household, but better-paid servants, such as the cook and butler, also bossed them.

The cook, a key servant in the household, could earn as much as £30 a year. The job was a tough one, however, for meals and snacks might be ordered at any time of the day or night, and our Edwardian ancestors ate huge amounts. In large households there were under-cooks and kitchen maids to help prepare the food.

The man responsible for the servants was the butler. He answered the door, checked the behaviour and dress of the maids and menservants, and looked after the family at meals. A trusted butler became almost a friend of the family.

While the lady of the house enjoyed her own bath, servants made do with a jug and basin in their room.

12

The maid's room was often in the attic at the top of the house. It was usually very cold and had little furniture.

IN THE HOUSE

Many of the gadgets that we take for granted were not available to the Edwardians. Electric light was a new invention, so many homes still used gas lighting or even candles, which made the rooms stuffy and dirty. The risk of fire was considerable.

Heating was usually produced by

A 'Baby Daisy' vacuum cleaner.

An electric reading lamp.

open wood or coal fires in every room. These had to be cleaned and kept burning by the servants — in a large house this was a full-time job for at least one maid. The lady of the house would not get up in the winter until the maid had prepared a good blaze in her bedroom grate, and she would ring for the maid at any time just to put a lump of coal on the fire.

used for all washing purposes.

Compared with today, the interiors of Edwardian houses were gloomy and heavy. Furniture was made of dark stained wood. Carpets and curtains were sombre and dull. The Edwardian middle class felt such furnishings were elegant and tasteful.

By the 1900s, the telephone had become a popular way of communicating over long distances, but not every rich home had one.

This parlaphone is the Edwardian version of a record player.

Large houses had a bell pull in the corner of each room. This was connected by wires to a bell board in the servants' quarters, enabling them to tell in which room the bell had been rung. When the bell sounded, woe betide the servant who dawdled.

While some homes had telephones, very few had vacuum cleaners, so in most households the servants had to do all the sweeping with dustpan and brushes. There were no aerosols or special cleaners: ordinary soap was

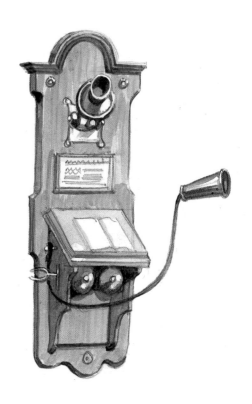

COOKING AND FOOD

Well-to-do Edwardians ate well. The example was set by the king himself, who regularly ate a massive breakfast, an eight-course lunch and a ten-course supper in the evening. The servant-owning middle class could not afford such gluttony, but they did enjoy good food, as this menu of a comfortably-off family with four servants shows:

Breakfast: Porridge, fried bacon and eggs, bread, butter, toast, marmalade, coffee, tea, milk, cream.

Dinner: Mutton, carrots, turnips, caper sauce, potatoes, hay-rick pudding, lemon sauce, tapioca pudding, tea.

| Tea: | Bread, butter, cereal, marmalade, milk, cream, tea. |
| Supper: | Cutlets, stewed plums, bread, biscuits, cheese, cocoa. |

The servants 'below stairs' did not eat so well. They were given three plain meals a day, but they could also finish up the food left over from the feasts upstairs — and perhaps even the wine. Many of the upper and middle classes were overweight, especially the men: a fat servant was not very common.

Cooking was still mostly done in heavy iron pots on iron ovens, heated by coal or coke. Some homes had a new oil stove. The very well-off had refrigerators. All grinding, mixing, grating and blending in the kitchen had to be done by hand. There were no packets or frozen meals, and tinned foods were scarce, so each recipe had to be prepared from scratch, using the original individual ingredients. Dishes took ages to create, but tasted delicious.

The kitchen was always busy; after breakfast, lunch had to be prepared.

CLOTHING

Servants in Edwardian times wore smart, formal clothes. A maid had a long, dark dress with a tight-fitting waist and a high neck, over which she wore a white apron. On her feet she wore lace-up boots. Her hair was tied

While the upper class wore silk and wool, the servants' dress was designed to be practical. Aprons were made of thick cotton, which was easy to wash and keep clean.

up and many households expected her to wear a little white cap.

Menservants wore clothes much like today's, except that they preferred boots to shoes, and more often than not wore a cap (outdoors) and a waistcoat. The butler was different. He dressed in a black tails suit, such as we see at some weddings, and his stiff shirt was topped with a wing collar and tie.

The gowns of rich ladies were exquisite. Tight at the waist, they flowed to the ground in elegant folds. From the waist to the high neckline, there was an intricate mixture of lace, frills and tucks. Broad hats were much in fashion. Beneath the dresses they wore petticoats and tightly laced bodices, designed to give shape to ladies whose figures were no longer in their prime. The wealthy had all their clothes made specially for them.

Men of the middle class wore suits: tweed ones for informal days and black for work and evening wear, when they also had wing collars on their shirts. Hats varied with the occasion: bowlers were normal wear, top hats appeared on special occasions, caps were worn for shooting, and in the summer fashionable young men sported light straw boaters.

HEALTH

COTES WARD LONDON HOSPITAL

At the beginning of this century the British were not a healthy race. In 1903 the Director General of the Army Medical Service estimated that six out of every ten men were unfit for military service. But there was a tremendous difference between the working classes and the wealthier sections of society.

This Edwardian hospital in London provided basic care for working-class people.

Diseases that are now less common, such as tuberculosis or typhoid, still killed thousands, particularly among the under-nourished poor. Surgery was very dangerous: Edward VII was one of the first men to have his appendix removed, and many thought that he would die on the operating table. The rich diet of the wealthy was not very good for their health either.

There was no National Health Service in Edwardian times. Hospitals were regarded as places for the poor: richer families were treated at home. The middle classes could afford doctors, and considerate employers would usually pay their servants' medical expenses. But if an employee became too ill to work and had to leave her job, sometimes there was nowhere to go but the workhouse.

Dentistry was not yet a serious profession: both rich and poor had painful teeth extracted with pliers. Only the family in a household took baths regularly, and the servants had to make do with jugs of water carried to their bedrooms. At the end of a long day they were probably too tired even for that.

The upper classes ate well, too well in fact. Rich sickly food and little exercise often led to heart complaints and gout.

CHILDHOOD

In Edwardian times attitudes towards children were changing. In most middle-class households they were no longer regarded as creatures to be seen and not heard. Beatrix Potter's stories were written in this period, as were *Winnie the Pooh* and *The Wind in the Willows*. These and other delightful books show that children were regarded with much love. For lucky children of wealthy parents there were also beautifully made toys and games.

Households that could afford it hired a nanny, who the children saw more often than their own parents. Nanny looked after their health and their clothes; she washed and bathed them, and took them for walks.

Many Edwardian children became

Rich children were looked after by a nanny, who often took them to the park.

closely attached to their nannies, sometimes caring for them in their old age with considerable affection. When the children were four or five some parents hired a governess or tutor to start their schooling. They were not looked upon so kindly as nanny was.

Servants could not keep their own children in the household. A maid who had a baby had to leave service. Life for the children of the working classes was hard. They were usually hungry and poorly clothed. The street was the only place for them to play.

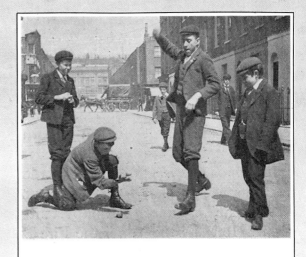

For working-class children the streets were their playground. Here, they are playing with spinning tops.

GOING TO SCHOOL

By Edwardian times all children between the ages of 5 and 14 had to attend school. Free elementary schools were run by local councils, but in many areas children went to church schools. By 1914 most schools served cheap meals, and gave free medical treatment for poor children.

In some elementary schools there was only one teacher for every fifty pupils, and senior boys and girls who were still at school had to help with

Free elementary schools were crowded. There are over 40 children in this classroom.

the teaching. They were called pupil-teachers. Much of the work was very boring and included plenty of learning by heart: pupils were beaten if they misbehaved or forgot their work. Most students left school able to read and write, but not much more.

Many middle-class families looked down on local elementary schools. They did not want their children to go to the same school as the servants' children, so they paid school fees for their children to be privately educated. For the wealthy this education started at home with the

Middle-class children were often taught at home by a governess.

governess. Then, at the age of 8, boys and girls were sent away to board at preparatory schools, before going on to a public school until the age of 18.

Children of poorer parents almost always had to leave school at 14 because they could not afford to stay on. In 1914 there were only 70,000 free secondary school places in the whole country. In schooling, as in the household, the Edwardians were a divided people.

25

CHURCH AND CHAPEL

Many middle-class Edwardian households felt it important to go to church on Sundays. But even here men and women were separated by class. A farmworker's boy remembers what it was like: 'My mother was a person of the lower class . . . She and her friends were all poor. They had to sit in the back pews. In the middle of the church were the local shopkeepers and people who were considered to be a little bit superior to the others — better educated perhaps. And right at the top of the church . . . were the local farmers, the local bigwigs, you see. Posh people.'

Quite a few middle-class families, especially in the towns, did not bother to go to church. Some of them felt very angry about religion and joined societies which attacked Christianity in newspapers and debates.

The church played an important part in the lives of some Edwardians.

The working classes of the cities rarely went to church, but in some parts of the country, such as Wales, they attended chapel regularly. Here the sermons were more lively and there was always plenty of cheerful singing.

A servant who lost his or her job might well have had to rely on the Salvation Army for help. This Christian group worked in the cities, feeding and finding shelter for the poor and homeless. Many poor Edwardians owed their lives to its kindness.

RECREATION

The range of entertainments available for an Edwardian servant-owning family was colossal. At home they read, played cards, made music, or had parties with friends. There was no radio or television, but fashionable households had one of the new gramophones.

If the family went out, there were concerts and plays to see; sports were increasingly popular, too. Golf and tennis were the best liked by the middle classes. Holidays by the sea were an annual event, while the upper classes regularly took trips abroad.

The servants did not have such

Swimming and making sand-castles were all part of a trip to the seaside.

good opportunities for recreation as their masters. In the house there was little to do but read, sew or play cards in their spare time. On days off they might go to the pub or the music hall. Professional sport was also growing rapidly: one hundred thousand spectators regularly attended the Cup Final at the Crystal Palace in London. The most modern entertainment was the cinema. The black and white films were silent, a suitable musical accompaniment being played by a pianist at the front of the hall.

In 1876 the *Daily Mail* newspaper was launched. Selling at only ½d a copy, it was the first newspaper especially designed to appeal to a wider readership. Upstairs the family preferred *The Times*, while below stairs they enjoyed the well-illustrated *Mail*.

Tennis was a popular middle-class game. Tennis fashions, as we can see, were different from today's.

1914

On 4 August 1914, Britain declared war on Germany, so joining the First World War. When the fighting ended on 11 November 1918, the country had changed tremendously. Millions of men had been killed and wounded, and the government finally had to give the vote to women, who had done so much on farms and in factories to help in the war effort.

The comfortable confidence of the Edwardian middle classes was shattered. Taxes rose, servants asked for higher wages and within twenty five years only the very wealthy could afford to have their housework done for them by others. The Edwardian household, with its luxury and un-fairness, was gone for ever.

This painting of the front line in 1915 is by John Nash. Many young lives were lost in the First World War.

GLOSSARY

Aristocrat   A member of the upper class; a noble.

Boater   A flat straw hat.

Bridge   A card game.

Dialect   The way people speak in a particular area.

Drawing room   A room where people used to go after dinner.

Lintel   A thick supporting stone placed over a door or window.

Manual work   Work done by hand.

Omnibus   The old word from which we get the word 'bus'.

Parlour   A small sitting room.

Pew   A bench seat in a church.

Population   The number of people living somewhere.

Public school   Fee-paying school.

Slum   A dirty, run-down house or street.

Sombre   Dark and gloomy.

Terraced houses   Houses joined together in rows.

Wing collar   A turned-up collar with just the points folded down.

Workhouse   A building where the homeless poor were housed and found work.

MORE BOOKS TO READ

Nance Lui Fyson, *Growing Up in Edwardian Britain* (Batsford, 1980).

Robert Hoare, *Turn of the Century* (Macdonald, 1975).

Christopher Martin, *The Edwardians* (Wayland, 1974).

Sallie Purkis, *At Home and in the Street in 1900* and *At School and in the Country in 1900* (Longman, 1981).

Alan Delgado, *Edwardian England* (Longman, 1967).

INDEX

Picture acknowledgements

The pictures in this book were supplied by the following: The Imperial War Museum 30; The Mansell Collection 5, 12, 23; Mary Evans Picture Library 6, 20, 24, 29.
32